A Scots Song

A
Scots Song
A Life of Music

James MacMillan

BIRLINN

First published in 2019 by
Birlinn Limited
West Newington House
10 Newington Road
Edinburgh
EH9 1QS
www.birlinn.co.uk

ISBN 978 178027 617 5

British Library Cataloguing in Publication Data
A catalogue record for this book is available from
the British Library.

Designed and typeset by Mark Blackadder

Printed and bound by Bell & Bain Limited, Glasgow

Contents

For Lynne, Catherine,
Aidan and Clare

Chapter 1

Musical Roots

Mass can be pretty tedious for young kids, and by the time I was five or six, I was bored with my weekly practice at home. I could never see very much, for a start, apart from the backs of heads, and I used to crawl around my parents' legs, creating mayhem and mischief with my sister Suzanne. In the 1960s, we used to visit my aunt and uncle in Edinburgh, and it was at Mass in St Mary's Metropolitan Cathedral in York Place that I was struck by something different and unusual – a ghostly, distant and affecting sonic concoction that gripped my childish attention. I strained my neck above the crowd in the pews in front of me. I couldn't see much from the back rows, but what I heard was clearly connected to the hazy images I could just make out at the other end of the building.

What could I see? Stylised movements of adults and children in robes, clouds of smoke and actions of devotion that I didn't yet comprehend. The sound was accompanying, facilitating. Looking back on it, and knowing now what liturgy is, I must have been hearing polyphony and Gregorian chant.

I later discovered that the choirmaster at St Mary's in the 1960s was none other than Arthur Oldham, founder of the Edinburgh Festival Chorus and a friend (and the only composition pupil) of Benjamin Britten. He had come to Edinburgh and converted to Catholicism a few years before I visited the Cathedral. He then took up the directorship of the Cathedral choir, which, under his charge, had become one of the finest in the land, impressing the likes of Carlo Maria Giulini and Georg Solti, who invited the choir to perform at the International Festival. Oldham was one of the first musicians in Scotland to reintroduce Scottish pre-Reformation music such as Robert Carver's 19-part motet *O bone Jesu*, and he gave the first Scottish performances of Benjamin Britten's *Missa Brevis*.

Considering what I was to do with my own life in the decades ahead, these unexpected formative early encounters with music in the Cathedral seem like happy accidents. I'm writing this short book as I approach my sixtieth birthday and look ahead to August 2019, when the Edinburgh International Festival will celebrate my music and my long-held relationship with the Festival through a series of special performances across the city. My childhood experiences in Edinburgh and, in a more sustained way, back home in the working-class communities of Cumnock and East Ayrshire were seminal for me, shaping and moulding much of what I have done in my music and in my other activities, and in how I have thought about life and art in the years since. In this book, I want to share the things that have proved vital in my work – an inescapable search for the sacred, the role of religious practice, tradition and identity, the influence of political motivation, for good or for ill, and the importance of music in the communities I hold dear.

*   *   *

Music and spirituality are very closely entwined. They have a centuries-long relationship through the Church, and some of the great music of our civilisation has been written for divine worship. But even in modernity, when the master–servant contract between ecclesial authorities and composers has been broken, music continues its reach into the crevices of the human–divine experience. Music has the power to look into the abyss as well as to the transcendent heights. It can trigger the most severe and conflicting extremes of feeling, and it is in these dark and dingy places – where the soul is probably closest to its source, where it has its relationship with God – that music can spark life that has long lain dormant.

Some claim that all music is sacred, not just the stuff that is written for liturgy. When people, including agnostics and atheists, say that 'music is the most spiritual of the arts', they are accounting for the impact it has on their lives – its power to affect not just emotions but also relationships and ways of seeing the world, and the events which mark our individual and personal journeys. Music is able to 'speak' to the soul in a way that goes beyond what words and images can convey. I continue to have a relationship with the Church – I write music for its liturgy, but it's not the main thing I do in my life. I spend a lot of my time with non-religious music-lovers with whom I share a fascination for and devotion to serious music. We are involved in a joint journey of discovery which takes us somewhere beyond ourselves, and which allows us to see ourselves as significantly more than the sum of our parts. Is that what makes music spiritual? No doubt we will have many different perspectives on this.

My instinct is that the secular and the sacred are inextricably connected, and that for me, my journey as a composer began in those distant snatches of Gregorian chant and Palestrina motets which floated down from the sanctuary of St Mary's in the mid 1960s. I have a special place in my heart for plainchant. It has a timeless, numinous and soothing quality, of course – a kind of perfect, unending melody. And I am not surprised it has gained renewed popularity in the secular world. In the Western art tradition it has always been the root of music, inspiring composers from the Middle

Ages onwards and shaping the nature of the song of the Church for centuries.

Even in the modern world, chant continues to inspire. My old friend and mentor, the now departed Peter Maxwell Davies, always had a copy of the *Liber Usualis* (the major compendium of Gregorian chant) on his desk. He was proud of this. He would delve into it, just for musical and spiritual sustenance, and sometimes music would emerge from his contemplations of it. He was no friend of the Church but, like many secular music lovers, he respected the roots of our musical, artistic and philosophical culture in Judeo-Christian civilisation.

My own rootedness in this civilisation had a lot to do with my family and the small community of Catholics in the Ayrshire mining town of Cumnock. The core of this community was the local parish church of St John the Evangelist, designed by William Burges for the third Marquess of Bute and constructed between 1878 and 1880. My parents were both baptised in St John's as children and then married there in 1958. I was baptised there a year later, received the other Sacraments throughout the 1960s and played the church's organ as a teenager.

The local primary school of St John's had been served for decades throughout the twentieth century by the Sisters of the Sacred Hearts of Jesus and Mary. They educated me and, most importantly, arranged for Miss Gray, our classroom music teacher, to distribute a batch of plastic recorders to the children of Primary 5 one day in 1968. This event was like a light going on for me; from that day I knew I wanted to be involved in and create music. It wasn't long before I was playing the piano, the trumpet and cornet and being pressed into service by the nuns at St John's to accompany classroom hymns.

Central to my early encouragement in music was my maternal grandfather, George Loy. He was a coal miner all his life, like many men in the area, and spent his fifty-odd working years underground, but his main passion was music. He played euphonium in colliery bands and was a dedicated choir member at St John's all through the 1930s, '40s and '50s. He introduced my mother Ellen to music when she was young, and she studied the piano and played until she married my dad. But her heart was never really in it. So when I came along, my grandfather was greatly pleased. He got me my first cornet and took me to band practices in nearby Dalmellington. He was keen for me to start playing the organ for Mass and bought me a basic organ tutor and a set of hymn books, which were pressed into service in due course.

The British composer can seem an odd beast to our mainland European counterparts. First of all, many think we only write 'pastoral' music, and they don't just mean Ralph Vaughan Williams and Gerald Finzi. They even detect this musical and aesthetic 'defect' in the likes of Harrison Birtwistle. I suppose I do too – there is a profound melancholic sigh in much British musical modernism that can be traced back some generations – but I don't think it's defective. And there is something else that we Brits do that many mainland European composers can't get their heads around – we write serious music for amateurs as well as professionals. From Vaughan Williams and Holst, to Britten, Tippett and Maxwell Davies, we have valued the role of the non-specialist in the nation's musical life. This has led many of our composers to create significant works for amateur choirs, local bands, workers' collectives and children. Some of the mainland European composers think this is beneath them (they've told me so!), and this may explain their dismissive attitude to us as musical dilettantes.

Nothing could be further from the truth. Amateur music-making is the jewel in the British crown and vital to the musical ecology of these islands, as can be seen in the number of flourishing composer-led festivals that have sprung up here over the decades. Aldeburgh was established by Benjamin Britten in 1948, and community music-making, including the composition of new operas for local children to perform, was an essential ingredient in its blossoming success. Peter Maxwell Davies created the St Magnus International Festival in 1977, and a similar pattern emerged there too. I remember attending some of the early festivals as an undergraduate, trekking up to Orkney with a two-man tent and hardly any money. Max was keen from the start that the local people would have both ownership and input into the proceedings. A Festival Chorus was formed from the people on the islands, and it performed in church and village halls alongside visiting orchestras and some of the world's great musicians. Max wrote new works all the time, a number of these for local performers, including his children's opera *Cinderella*, the premiere of which I attended in 1980.

As the years went by and my own creative life developed I sometimes wondered if I would ever start a similar festival myself and where it might be. One of the most important lectures I ever heard as a student was from the ethnomusicologist Peter Cooke of the School of Scottish Studies at the University of Edinburgh. He asked us to make a note of all the places in our town or village where music was made. I began to think of the various different functions music had in the lives of ordinary people, in ordinary places. Amateur music-making was a major feature of life in working-class Ayrshire throughout the twentieth century, and in Cumnock, where the main industry was coal-mining, the brass and silver band tradition was strong. There was also a fine music club, where I heard performances given by the Berlin Philharmonic Octet (made up of players from the Berlin

Philharmonic Orchestra), Leon Spierer, the concertmaster of the same, and prominent chamber musicians from all over the country. I met a lot of the performers and volunteered to turn pages for the pianists in their recitals.

There was a social and communitarian dimension to music-making, and it was also closely tied to rituals, some religious, but not all – music filled the dance halls and working men's clubs where courtship rituals were played out and local folk and pop bands entertained. Singing societies worked hard all year round, preparing amateur operatic works and standard oratorio performances by composers including Handel, Stainer, Gilbert and Sullivan and Rodgers and Hammerstein.

All these early memories fed my decision to establish my own festival in my old home town. The Cumnock Tryst launched in 2014 with a choral concert given by The Sixteen, conducted by Harry Christophers, in the church where my grandfather and I had aided the liturgy, two generations apart. The violinist Nicola Benedetti, who grew up in Ayrshire, is our patron, and in 2016 her piano trio came to the festival with performances of Brahms and Ravel that I have never heard surpassed. The King's Singers have been too, and in 2017 we were joined by Scottish Ensemble as well as the choir of Westminster Cathedral and star soloists Colin Currie, percussionist, and Sean Shibe, guitarist.

The brass theme continues year on year. At the 2017 festival, the Dalmellington Band was conducted by Martyn Brabbins, a band trombonist turned conductor who is now director of English National Opera. Like St Magnus Festival, we have also established a Festival Chorus, conducted by one of the most gifted choral trainers in the land, Eamonn Dougan, and it has covered Mozart, Fauré and Vaughan Williams so far. For the 2018 festival, I composed a new oratorio, *All the Hills and Vales Along*, especially for the Chorus and the Dalmellington Band, to mark the centenary of the Armistice of World War One. The performance in the Old Church of Cumnock included the Edinburgh Quartet and star tenor soloist Ian Bostridge. The Festival Chorus members love what we ask them to do, and our audience of locals and visitors grows each year. It seems a mad thing to embark on in my middle age, but I love it. All the great musicians I speak to about Cumnock have said yes to me so far, which is monumentally exciting, and up to now we have raised sufficient funds, though, like most arts organisations, we proceed with hopes and prayers.

We also work with local children and students, supporting them to create their own music, for which we offer a platform. Some of the children have additional support needs, and our work alongside Drake Music Scotland clearly demonstrates that disability is no barrier to either a love for or involvement in music. I sometimes come across people – they tend to be on the left, politically, but not always – who believe that complex, discursive music like classical and jazz isn't what ordinary working-class kids should be doing. If someone had told me and my parents this back in the day, we would have laughed in their faces. I remember Cumnock as a very musical place, where ordinary men and women from humble homes would make music together. There wasn't a lot of money around – many people were genuinely poor – but it's clear that this music-making at an early age can transform lives; it certainly changed mine.

A Scots Song

My path will be familiar to many of those who were working-class Scottish children of the 1960s and '70s. We were offered free music lessons and involvement in school orchestras, bands and choirs, and our teachers knew how to nurture our talents and enthusiasms into lifelong vocations and careers. These opportunities are now under threat in Scotland with the creep of additional fees for hard-pressed parents, as music-education budgets are being slashed by councils around the country. The effect of this is to discourage less well-off youngsters from joining the world of music. British orchestras are far more populated by musicians from affluent backgrounds (many of them privately educated) nowadays compared to even a generation ago, when sons of miners made up the brass sections of the great orchestras of the land.

A discursive music, which is complicated and requires focus and concentrated skill (like learning to play an instrument or singing), can take a lifetime's commitment, both for listeners and performers, as well as for composers, of course. But it is a lifetime that is full of rewards, artistically, emotionally, socially and intellectually. Active

engagement with music brings benefits throughout people's lives. Even very young children's
perceptual development is enhanced by musical
engagement – it promotes language development,
improves literacy and encourages rhythmic co-
ordination. Fine motor skills are honed by learning
to play an instrument. Participation in music also
seems to improve spatial reasoning, one aspect of
general intelligence that is related to some of the
skills required in mathematics. General attainment
is clearly affected by literacy and numeracy skills,
but involvement in music also appears to improve
self-esteem, self-efficacy and aspirations – all
important factors in improving young people's
commitment to studying and perseverance in
other subjects.

Why would those in power allow poorer children to miss out on such a vital ingredient of their
education? It's as if their sanctimonious mantras
about inclusion, access and diversity get thrown
straight out the window as soon as they are asked
to do something about it. During a period when
Scotland's government has increased spending on
education and culture, it seems perverse to cut

back on instrumental music education, which plays such an important role in narrowing the attainment gap and in the development of the whole child.

Great Scottish musicians are the evidence for the effectiveness of Scotland's music education, and they include many who may not have succeeded without an effective music tuition service, open to all regardless of ability to pay for lessons. John Wallace, trumpeter and former principal of the Royal Conservatoire of Scotland, says, 'I came from the wrong side of the tracks to the other side, because of music. Music is incredibly beneficial to social mobility.' It would be a severely retrograde step to deny the young people of today the opportunities their parents and grandparents once had.

The happy accidents which befell me – listening to the choir at St Mary's Cathedral in Edinburgh as a little boy, being handed a plastic recorder at St John's, talking with my grandfather – set me on a path towards a happy and fulfilling creative life in music. My hope is that The Cumnock Tryst will inspire more children in Ayrshire to follow their musical dreams.

Chapter 2

―❧―

Polyphonies

In 1973, I changed secondary schools from St Conval's High School to Cumnock Academy. It was tough and unusual at the time to jump from the local Catholic secondary to the neighbouring 'non-denominational', culturally Protestant, equivalent. There were raised eyebrows all round; my parents even got a stern letter from the Bishop of Galloway berating them for letting down the Catholic community. It was thought by some that we had turned our backs on the faith. Nothing was further from the truth. It was not theological reasons that motivated my parents' decision but far more mundane considerations about my curricular timetable – at Cumnock Academy, for instance, I was able to study Music as well as German. This kind of thing is handled much more sensibly and cooperatively in clutches of neighbouring schools today.

There were a few aggressive remarks and threats when I got to the 'Protestant school', but I learned whom to avoid and who were going to be good friends. The girls were especially nice and made me feel at home; Lynne Frew was one of the quieter ones, and quite shy. She always blushed noticeably when I spoke to her.

The strange thing about the move was that my interest in and love of Catholicism actually took off when I was there. I continued playing the organ for Mass in the town, and I could feel my interior spiritual life beginning to grow, mostly owing to geeky, teenage autodidacticism. The main factor in this spiritual search and maturation, though, was musical. Bert Richardson, the music teacher at my new school, introduced not just me but all my new 'Protestant' friends in the school choir to the glories of Renaissance and also Counter-Reformation polyphony.

For a few years, we were living on a diet of masses and motets by Palestrina, Lassus and Monteverdi. This was tempered by much Bach and Telemann too, for ecumenical balance, of course, but the damage had been done! We had all been inculcated into the beauties of Catholic music culture, right under the noses of the school authorities and parents. In fact, one of the first choral pieces I ever wrote was for the school choir – a Sanctus from my *Missa Brevis* from 1977, which I remember conducting at the Ayrshire Music Festival that year.

A number of romances began in Bert Richardson's choir, and many of them led, a few years later, to marriage. My sister Suzanne (soprano) married Stephen (bass), son of one of the local Church of Scotland ministers; Lynne Frew's younger brother Kelvin (tenor) married Wilma (soprano) from New Cumnock; my friend Allan (bass) married Lynne's best pal Mhairi (alto); and I (tenor) – as you might have guessed – married Lynne (alto).

The standard of performance was pretty good too – better than one might expect from a bunch of miners' and farmers' kids from remotest East

Ayrshire. There's a YouTube clip of our school choir singing Holst's 'Awake, Awake' on an STV religious programme from 1976 which is rather impressive. We all look ridiculous though – an embarrassing, car-crash mixture of long, heavy-metal hair and Scottish Presbyterian prim. Rather sweetly, in the video I'm standing next to Lynne, my then brand-new girlfriend.

A love of music, and singing especially, has lived with the members of the school choir, and I still see many of the old faces, now in their late fifties and older, cropping up in other choral groups. Many have joined The Cumnock Tryst Festival Chorus and only last year took part in the world premiere of *All the Hills and Vales Along*, which I composed for them. It was strange but heartwarming to see and hear all these people that I first met at Cumnock Academy still singing decades later.

Bert Richardson had been an organ student of George McPhee at the Royal Scottish Academy of Music. McPhee has spent most of his life as organist and choir director at Paisley Abbey and has performed a lot of Kenneth Leighton's music there and elsewhere. I developed a real love of the choral tradition through Richardson's influence and teaching, and, as a teenager, at special choral weekend courses led by McPhee, I got to know the twentieth-century expression of this music by composers such as Holst, Vaughan Williams, Kodaly and Britten. Kenneth Leighton's music also figured strongly in the affections and admirations of McPhee and Richardson, and I was excited that he was teaching at the University of Edinburgh. This was the main reason I chose to study there, and he was a marvellous teacher.

The Reid School's emphasis on the traditional, generic skills which Kenneth taught us – a diet of harmony, counterpoint, fugue, orchestration, ana-lysis – has somewhat waned in recent years, but it was an absolutely crucial foundation to my training as a composer. I worry that the new generation of composers may have missed out on this. Writing four- and five-part species counterpoint or three- and four-part fugal expositions, while certainly challenging, was a vital discipline that taught me so much about complexity and how to handle layers upon layers of music.

In 2018, I composed a forty-part motet, *Vidi*

Aquam, and I could feel Kenneth's presence over my shoulder all the time! He was no longer correcting my parallel fifths, but he was guiding the archetype. I think I inherited his love for making lines work in tandem with each other. Once you settle into work of this sort, it becomes engrossing and compelling; it sometimes feels like knitting, or doing crosswords. Some have commented on the conservative nature of Kenneth Leighton's music, but as a teacher he was very open to the more radical figures of the age. He knew and admired the work of Pierre Boulez, for example, and arranged for a performance of his *Le Marteau sans maître* in a university concert series when I was there as an undergraduate. In one memorable lesson, I remember Kenneth analysing a piano piece by Luigi Dallapiccola and showing how the Italian composer had transformed this into an orchestral work. It was a wonderful insight into orchestration and the beauties of contemporary colours and proved to be a lesson of fundamental importance to me. I look back at my four years as an undergraduate with Kenneth with immense gratitude and feel very lucky that I was able to saturate myself in the workings of music, past and present, under his guidance.

During my first days as a fresher in Edinburgh, I met Fr Aidan Nichols OP. He was the Catholic chaplain to the university, aged about twenty-seven at the time, and he asked me to form a schola to sing at the student Masses. He was to become one of the most important academic theologians in the English-speaking world and would author dozens of important and influential books. His very first book, *The Art of God Incarnate, Theology and Image in Christian Tradition*, was dedicated to the undergraduate me, 'amico dilecto in Christo'.

In 1978, he organised a summer tour to France for our choir, which, by this time, had acquired the ridiculously grand title of Schola Sancti Alberti Magni (after St Albert the Great, who is the patron of the Dominican Priory in George Square, Edinburgh). This sojourn has since been known as the Schola Disaster Tour. We hired two minibuses from the University of Edinburgh, and by the time we had reached the Midlands, heading south to the channel crossings, we had crashed one into the other. They were both write-offs. We had to begin again. Hiring two new minibuses at Dover, we crossed on the ferry, but by the time we reached Calais the big end had gone in one of them. We were stranded, a choir of thirty with one fifteen-seater minibus between us, with concerts looming in the next few days around northern France.

We had to borrow a lot of money from the various Dominican and Benedictine establishments we were staying at in Paris and elsewhere to limp around from one place to the next, half of us travelling unexpectedly by train. One concert that sticks in the mind was in Solesmes, a commune in the department of Sarthe. It is famous for its Benedictine monastery, which, from the early twentieth century, has been central to the renewal and spread of Gregorian chant, its related musicology and liturgy. The men of the choir were housed in monastery guest rooms; the women were all in a communal dormitory just outside the monastery grounds, as is the way in traditional Benedictine establishments. And I'm afraid to say that the men were treated royally by the monks, dined and wined in the refectory, while the women had to fend for themselves. One night they had to share one chicken between the fifteen of them. We realised that there might be some tension when they found out how well we had feasted, so we smuggled out bits of nougat from the end of the dinner to share with them. It was not appreciated . . .

It was only in the last years as students at Edinburgh that Lynne and I began to notice how poor we were compared to many of our student colleagues. I hadn't cared about this at all – musicians tend to be engrossed in the music to the point of being oblivious to everything else. But it was harder for Lynne to ignore in the Law Faculty. There was some serious money around some of the students there, noticeable especially at the time of faculty balls and dinners, which seemed out of bounds for us, unaffordable. Lynne's mum had brought her and her brother up on her own and had to be extremely vigilant with very meagre funds. My parents were together, but my dad was a joiner and there was always concern about finances, especially with a couple of children at university.

My mum's brother, my uncle Brian, was the first of our family to study at university, and it was a great aspiration among working-class families in the west of Scotland to achieve this academic and economic step-change. Brian had been a Labour councillor in the 1960s and '70s and had inherited his commitment to the Labour movement from his dad, my Papa George. I developed an interest in politics too as a teenager and followed family members to the Labour Party, even becoming a branch chairman and delegate to the Constituency Party in the mid 1980s. In retrospect, one might say that my premature interest in politics took a particularly militant turn with the romantic gesturalism of my teenage years.

For a time I fell under the spell of the extreme left, joining the Young Communist League when I was fourteen. This caused great pain to my grandfather, who had fought Marxists in the National Union of Mineworkers when they were in total support of the Soviet Union, Stalin and the horrific slaughter and repression visited on Russia and Eastern Europe in the mid century. He was upset at my decision, and both he and Uncle Brian tried to dissuade me. I was stubborn, though, and held my ground. Looking back on it, they were right – it was one of the worst things I've ever done. Decades later, I still wake up in a sweaty lather of guilt and mortification that I might have given succour to one of the most evil movements in human history. I was a teenager at the time, but still, the politics of the ultra-left infected and corroded me for years, before I gradually woke up and shed the virus. Politically, I feel that I haven't necessarily gone in the opposite direction; I'm mundanely non-descript in my positions, tediously middle-of-the-road, with an abiding tinge of the social restraint I had even when I was in the Communist Party, during which time I never abandoned my Catholic faith. Some think that is strange. Maybe it is. I remember attending a Communist weekend conference in Edinburgh when I was about sixteen and causing annoyance when I missed the Sunday-morning session to attend Mass at St Mary's Metropolitan Cathedral. I suppose even by that stage I had abandoned the cause.

Some throw insults and accusations at political agnostics like me, implying we are Conservatives. Even when I was in the Communist Party I was being accused of being a Tory! This points to a fatal self-destructive trait on the extreme left. I'm well shot of them. Others say that the left behave in a cultish way these days, as if their motivations were quasi-religious. I recognise that and therefore know what it must be like to be an agnostic. I have lost all my youthful certainties, and feel liberated as a result. One positive impact of losing one's religion (even an anti-religious religion like Marxism) is developing an ease and relaxation at being in the company and conversation of people who held or still hold different world views to one's own. Even today I read of Labour politicians claiming they could never be friends with someone from the other side of the tracks. How sad. Hearing other, different arguments and perspectives after freeing oneself from the clamps and strictures of camp loyalties was like stepping out of a prison. My reading changed, my friendships expanded. I would never have been able to engage with the ideas (and good company) of the likes of philosopher Roger Scruton, theologian George Weigel and sculptor Alexander Stoddart if I had not thrown off the chains of narrow ideological bitterness.

Does this political self-liberation have a musical

parallel? In his recent book *The Road To Somewhere*, David Goodhart talks about 'somewhere people' and 'anywhere people.' His analysis is a political one, of course, responding to recent developments in society and culture in the United Kingdom, the United States and elsewhere. But it made me wonder whether we can also talk about 'somewhere composers' and 'anywhere composers'. The reason we ask ourselves about a composer's sense of place today, geographically and stylistically, is due to the rise of a cosmopolitan, international aesthetic in musical modernism (and indeed postmodernism) which for many decades now has attempted to strain out any vestiges of localism (and tradition) in favour of a sophisticated, pannational contemporary music style.

When I attended the Internationale Ferienkurse für Neue Musik at Darmstadt in 1980, the Scandinavian music sounded very like the South American music, which sounded very like the Korean music, which sounded very like the German music, and on and on it went, round and round. The composers all prided themselves on this, and a particular ire was reserved for those who didn't fit the template. I remember Wolfgang Rihm's music being booed, mainly by other German composers, because it sounded German. The floating C-sharp-minor chords here and there brought memories of Mahler, perhaps. And they didn't like it. I was only a provincial undergraduate when I was there, and I couldn't work out why the Germans especially were accusing their country's greatest living composer of fascism and Nazism. It was clear, though, that the up-and-coming musical and cultural elites were setting out restrictions and guidelines on what new music should and should not be.

It is not necessarily reactionary and old-fashioned to be interested in, for example, the vernacular traditional music of one's own culture, or even someone else's. The Scottish composers who utilise local folk music in their work, for instance, don't do it as a genuflection to the past or as an obeisance to the way things used to be, but as a genuine search for new expressions. Think Judith Weir. Think James Dillon. Think Peter Maxwell Davies. And nor is it reactionary and old-fashioned to be open to a continual re-evaluation of musical traditions. Modernism, like Marxism, has brought renunciation and denunciation of the past. This has been perverse and destructive. The re-evaluation of musical traditions in my work is multi-faceted. Sometimes I've delved back into Scottish folk music; sometimes I've looked to the deep past and sometimes to my immediate predecessors in British music. The twentieth century saw an incredible flowering and opening up in art music on these islands, an astonishing proliferation of music with a healthy breadth of reference, of which Kenneth Leighton was a part. The influence of the mid-twentieth-century avant-garde turned many of us away from the major British composers who were judged to be outmoded. However, the careful and incisive advocacy of Benjamin Britten's music by the likes of Colin Matthews and Donald Mitchell dispelled the mean-mindedness at the heart of that particular criticism. Britten is a major international figure in modern music with a huge communica-tive reach in his operas, chamber music and orchestral scores. The same goes for his contem-porary Michael Tippett. Once these two regained favour, many began to look again with fresh eyes and ears at the musical world that had brought them forth and were willing to acknowledge the profundity, sophistication and beauty in the work of early twentieth-century English composers.

When I am invited to conduct abroad I am keen to include some of this music in my programmes. In Germany, France, Italy, and even in the United States, there is a lack of engagement with Elgar and Vaughan Williams. I enjoy taking this music to audiences who are relatively inexperienced in the British tradition, knowing that something unique may be communicated in these unexpected encounters. Conducting Vaughan Williams' Symphony No. 4 at the Grafenegg Festival in Austria and his *Fantasia on a Theme on Thomas Tallis* in Germany and Belgium were some of the highlights of my life as a conductor. The musicians and their audiences were surprised and beguiled by music they had heard about, but which had remained hazy, unexplored territory until these performances.

And there are separate trends of renunciation and denunciation in Scotland too. Before British-ness and Anglo-centricity became targets recently, it was pre-Reformation Scotland that got the forced-forgetting cold shoulder. It's strange that a culture so proud of its own history and character and fond of trumpeting its own Scottish exceptionalism is strangely mute about John Barbour, Robert Henryson and William Dunbar. It's as if patriotic modern Scotland is embarrassed or bewildered by its Catholic beginnings. The same might explain why we have never truly celebrated Robert Carver, one of Europe's greatest sixteenth-century composers, who has a special place in my heart and just happened to be Scottish. Influenced by composers in continental Europe, it is thought that he might even have travelled to Rome and the Netherlands in the learning of his craft. Highly ornate in style, decorative and polyphonically dense, his work resembles most closely the rich, glorious music of the Eton Choirbook. Carver proffers a fond memory of Scotland's Catholic roots and a signal of musical depth and complexity that can inspire composers like me today. I've quoted from and alluded to his ten-part *Missa Dum Sacrum Mysterium* in my fourth symphony as an homage from one Scottish composer to another, and I have walked in his footsteps by composing my own setting of 'O bone Jesu', inspired by his glorious, rich and teeming nineteen-part motet of the same name.

The polyphonic glories of pre- and post-Reformation history, first encountered in Bert Richardson's choir in Cumnock, enhanced by the analytical probings of Kenneth Leighton in Edinburgh and now given full vent in the work I am creating for the likes of Harry Christopher's heavenly choir, The Sixteen, have offered inspiration and artistic liberation for me. Shedding the pseudo-Marxist restrictiveness of academic and cosmopolitan modernism has indeed been a cultural parallel to my political journey. This is a renunciation of my own perhaps, but it has been exciting and provocative. I love writing music, and I am genuinely hungry and thirsty to know what will next be round the corner.

Chapter 3

Finding a Voice

After graduation in Edinburgh in 1981 it was time to find a teacher who would be good for me. There seemed something quite mediaeval in the way that young composers sought out a 'master' to help them develop their skills and technique. The choice of institution was secondary; more crucial was the nature of the teacher – their style, their aesthetic, their approach to the technical and practical issues of composition. I found mine just over the border at the University of Durham. John Casken was about ten years older than me, almost to the day, and was beginning to make his mark as one of the more individually defined young voices of an English modernism in the 1980s. Like Nigel Osborne, he had studied in Poland at a time when the likes of Witold Lutosławski and Krzysztof Penderecki were signalling a vital creativity in new music there. John had returned home to important commissions and performances, and word was getting around academia that he was an inspiring teacher.

And so it proved. At that stage, I needed an open-minded, non-doctrinaire figure who could communicate an intellectual shaping of modernism and encourage individual personality to develop in my work. There are different approaches to the issue of contemporary music. In the 1980s, there were still vestiges in the Academy of the strictly forbidding modernism I discussed in the last chapter, which had turned its back on references to tradition. This meant that there was a bias against tonality, for example, and anything that smacked of the past. The 'guardians' of avant-garde purity were always on the lookout for failings that needed to be purged. Anything that referenced the past, and especially the recent past of nineteenth-century romanticism (and popular styles) was anathema, and to be rooted out.

The twentieth century had seen, for various reasons, a retreat by the composing community from the larger music-loving public. In a period when audiences were becoming more conservative and less interested in the music of their own time, composers were going into exploratory mode. Around the turn of the century, Arnold Schoenberg had established a private society for the performance of new music. It was made up of the cognoscenti – those in the know when it came to the newest ideas in music – and insiders – other composers, musicologists and critics. The larger audience outside, it was thought, could not be trusted to understand the new musical languages.

That is one way of looking at it. Another is that the new trends became dominated by one particular view of what modernism should be – a view that placed the ideas of Schoenberg and his allies at the forefront of musical development and endeavour. Other modernisms were edged out. Would the history of twentieth-century music have been different if the dominant thrusts had preferred Leoš Janáček, for example, rather than Schoenberg?

A particular European modernism, with its roots in the Second Viennese School and developed by a small group of post-war composers in certain European towns and cities, has been given a special place in official understandings of the development of modern music. There was the sense that composers, and indeed the musical public, were to regard this sanctioned path as not just the way forward, but also the way things should be. State broadcasters, many sharing the aesthetic and political perspective of the composers themselves and their followers, gave the oxygen of publicity and dissemination to this view of the musical present and future.

This has been especially the case in Germany and France, where there is a centralised and top-down view of what high culture should be. A central, pivotal figure in this development was Pierre Boulez, a composer, conductor and radically scathing polemicist, at least in his younger days. An alpha male par excellence in the musical world, a powerful, driven figure, always manoeuvring politically and pushing boundaries imaginatively, he never hid his determination to put his biases into operation. It has been suggested that his influence on legions of third-rate imitators over the last few generations has been pernicious. Mediocre acolytes were bedazzled by the master's encyclopaedic panoply of colouristic subtleties and rhythmic intricacies – so much so that a lot of modern music is obsessed, fetishistically, with surface detail – to the detriment, perhaps, of core profundities.

Nevertheless, Boulez's influence on musical culture as a composer and a conductor was powerful and meticulously plotted. His choice of repertoire was large and interesting, covering Berlioz, Debussy, Ravel, Stravinsky, Bartók, Schoenberg and Messiaen. Others were constantly and steadily added – Wagner, Mahler and some major contemporary figures such as Luciano Berio and György Ligeti. But the omissions from this list are also fascinating and revealing. According to Boulez, Schumann, for example, showed 'little invention and even little skill'. Explaining his priorities, Boulez says, 'There are composers who possess this gift of instrumental invention and others who, more or less, lack it [. . .] If you compare the symphonies of Brahms with the operas of Wagner solely from the viewpoint of instrumentation [. . .] one is not bowled over by his [Brahms's] instrumental imagination.'

To my mind, the phrase 'solely from the viewpoint of instrumentation' is key here. Brahms's structural genius in reshaping classical models, his gift for soaring melody and expansive spiritual vision are all subordinated, by Boulez, to the ear-tickling skill of instrumental choice. Granted, Boulez came from a tradition that has emphasised perfumed delicacies and nuanced subtleties; this may explain not only his blind spots, but also modernism's over-indulgence of surfaces instead of the deep heart. Perhaps this justifies Boulez's disregard of Anton Bruckner, Paul Hindemith and Jean Sibelius, as well as all the Russians from Sergei Prokofiev and Dmitri Shostakovich to Alfred Schnittke. It may also explain the Anglophobic prejudices of many French musicians – for instance, Britten and Tippett never appeared in Boulez's repertoire, and only a few British composers who came after them do so. But there are also significant French omissions – Francis Poulenc, for instance, and any of the important contemporary figures that followed a different aesthetic, such as Henri Dutilleux. As far as American music is concerned, Boulez eschewed Aaron Copland and John Adams but embraced Elliott Carter. All conductors are discriminating, of course, and subjective preferences are widespread. But there was a ruthlessly ambitious personal agenda at work here. The music that Boulez said opened up 'new terrain', his emphasis on colour in Mahler, for instance, or his focus on rhythmic and melodic fragmentation in Anton Webern – all these point back to Boulez himself. He cunningly re-interpreted significant developments in music into self-justifying and self-aggrandising proto-modernism.

I have observed a very different kind of modern music culture in this country and, in different ways, in other parts of the Anglosphere, particularly in the United States in part. A plurality of aesthetics and styles has been valued in these places; there is no comparable intellectual restrictiveness or megalomania at work. It makes me think that different places experience the challenge of modernity in the arts in different ways. From the perspective of the

United States, for example, one sees radically alternative trajectories and a completely different range of personalities at the core of recent musical history. And who is to say that this narrative is less authentic than the official European one?

Common to both Europe and the New World were Stravinsky and Schoenberg, but their embrace of North American culture in the flight from European hostility is crucial. Shortly after Schoenberg's death, his widow found a note written in 1944 when the composer was living in Los Angeles and teaching at UCLA:

'There is a great man living in this country – a composer. He has solved the problem how to preserve one's self and to learn. He responds to negligence by contempt. He is not forced to accept praise or blame. His name is Ives.'

Charles Ives was the first great non-European modernist, and it is argued that he owed nothing of his originality to Europe. Although he is much celebrated now in modernist circles, it is as a great eccentric and one-off that the 'central orthodoxy' prefers to see him, a bit like Olivier Messiaen. But his great experiments in polytonality, polyrhythm, tone clusters, aleatoricism (creating music randomly) and quarter tones come from a different place philosophically and sociologically from those generated later in France, Germany and Italy. Fundamental to everything in Ives's imagination were hymn tunes and traditional songs, patriotic songs, the sentimental pop songs of the day, the melodies of Stephen Foster, the music of the dance halls and American popular culture – in fact, everything that the European liberal elites would later come to despise.

My discussions with John Casken about all of this in the 1980s proved to be important for me. He seemed to have a similar reluctance to be taken in by the grand narrative of musical modernism. He encouraged me to look to the peripheries. For John, his periphery had been Poland, and, no doubt as a result of being separated from Western Europe by the Iron Curtain, all the unexpected musical things that had happened there after the war. He also encouraged me to reassess the significance of the post-war European avant-garde.

Just think how a young composer in mainland Europe must have viewed the world in 1945, emerging from war, fascism and the Holocaust. It must have felt as if the old world had failed and deserved to be ditched. For many composers, musical tradition became regarded as flawed: as with all European bourgeois traditions, it had, so they said, led to the Third Reich and mass destruction, to the end of culture. Culture, art, music – all needed to begin again – with a blank page, so that this pure, virgin territory could be shaped by the new generation, and made better.

This outlook prevailed in philosophy and politics as well as in the arts, and one can understand how it gained traction, especially among young idealists. We can never forget that the Holocaust was committed by people from one of the great Western civilisations, one like ours, people who cultivated their fine artistic tastes in music and other forms. The house at Wannsee was the lovely, serene setting for a conference devoted to planning the world's greatest crime, and it was typical for the Nazis to surround themselves with beautiful scenery and architecture, classical music and books. Some of the most notorious Nazi concentration camps were constructed in scenic locations and had incongruous features including flower gardens, birdhouses, orchestras, a library, a zoo, and a swimming pool. Many cultured men and women today talk in elevated terms of the spirituality of the arts, and even of the arts filling the vacuum vacated by religion in the modern world. But there are lessons from recent history which should make us wary of these ideas, as George Steiner suggested: 'We now know that a man can read Goethe or Rilke in the evening, that he can play Bach and Schubert, and go to his day's work at Auschwitz in the morning.'

Theodor Adorno argued that after the atrocities of World War Two, it was barbaric to attempt to write poetry, that art could never be a guarantee of empathy or morality or even civilisation: 'That [Auschwitz] could happen in the midst of the philosophical traditions, the arts and the enlightening sciences says more than just that these failed to take hold of and change the people. All culture after Auschwitz, including its urgent critique, is rubbish.'

The philosopher Alasdair MacIntyre suggests that the apparent failures of the 'Enlightenment Project' to provide a rational underpinning to our moral life were not just the failures of its most distinguished intellectuals, but also that its values cannot be disentangled from the iron fist of progressive politics. Think of the revolutionary violence and terror of the French Revolution – a terror which attempted to replace God with Revolutionary Man, emptying the churches of the images of Jesus and his mother and replacing them with the gods and goddesses of the future. It didn't take long for 'new, improved Man' to unleash the violence inherent in the new creed across Europe, and this was to happen time and time again in the centuries ahead.

In fact, our still-fashionable view that humans can be perfected is the very reason our culture has been able to produce Auschwitz and will continue to do so until humanity embraces a truly radical counter-ontology. Centuries of Enlightenment culture failed to predict and prevent the forces of fascism and eugenics; this is an implacable indictment of that culture. And remember that eugenics was very popular among the liberal, civilised bien pensants of the United States, the United Kingdom and Scandinavia before the Nazis got excited about it. It's still overtly on the agenda today in the modern world's obsession with screening out disabilities.

Instead of a year-zero, end-of-culture return to the blank page, though, perhaps what was needed was a realistic review of history and culture since the French Revolution. I felt that a bracing and useful pessimistic approach to the bogus optimisms which brought us fascism, communism and Nazism in the twentieth century might also be useful in our reappraisals of artistic modernisms. What would this mean for a composer?

Even in my twenties, I was becoming aware of emerging 'heresies' challenging the post-war orthodoxies in new music. Composers were edging into new territories – some of which involved engaging with non-European cultures, minimalism, and various forms of rediscovery – of tonality, expression, tradition, vernacular musics and religion. Minimalism was a game-changer for many. I was entranced by much of it. Some of it, by the likes of Arvo Pärt, John Tavener and Henryk Górecki, delved into spiritual realms and others, such as Louis Andriessen, John Adams and Steve Martland, engaged with popular forms. These composers undoubtedly had an effect on me, so that by the time my first public commissions were beginning to appear, the bright tonalities, the driving rhythms, the explorations of extremes of serenity and violence, and the desire to communicate were finding their place in the likes of *Veni, Veni Emmanuel*, the percussion concerto I wrote for Evelyn Glennie, and, a few years before that, *The Confession of Isobel Gowdie*, which I wrote for the 1990 Proms.

I discovered the story of Isobel Gowdie on reading *The History of The Scottish People* by Scottish historian T.C. Smout. Although there may be some conjecture about the facts and significance of her life and death, it is clear that she was a real person, who lived near Nairn in the seventeenth century. In 1662, Isobel Gowdie confessed to having been baptised by the devil and joined a coven of thirteen who met at night; she had journeyed to the centre of the earth to feast with the king and queen of the fairies; she could fly, or become a hare, a cat or a crow; she used waxen images and bags of boiled toads to cause inflictions;

she had killed a ploughman with elf-arrows the devil gave her; and sometimes the devil beat her and raped her. She was subsequently strangled at the stake and burned in pitch amid scenes of hysterical fright and sadism.

The story is so vivid that the music could not help but be shaped and guided by some sense of narrative. This gave me cause for some reflection at the time. Why? Principally, because the orchestral tone poem, in all its picture-painting, story-telling implications, is a Romantic, nineteenth-century phenomenon, and it would surely be seen as odd that the form could be resurrected at the end of the twentieth century. Could it be done? And why would any 'modern' composer want to do it?

Initially I was drawn by the dramatic and programmatic potential of this terrible story but the work soon developed a far more emotional core as I attempted to draw together various strands in a single, complicated act of contrition. Rather grandiosely at the time, I imagined that, on behalf of the Scottish people, the work offered Isobel Gowdie the mercy and humanity that was denied her in the last days of her life. To do this I tried to capture the soul of Scotland in music, and the outer sections contain a multitude of chants, songs and litanies (real and imagined) coming together in a reflective outpouring – a prayer for the murdered woman. As with *Tryst*, which I wrote for the Scottish Chamber Orchestra, the *Confession* was infused with the modalities of Celtic music, pedal points like bagpipe drones, ornamentation and decorations from pibroch and Scots fiddle music, and the archetypal expressivity of Gaelic psalm-singing and Scots balladry.

In the years prior to the composition of the *Confession*, I had immersed myself in Scottish and Irish folk music, joining a few bands as a whistle player, keyboardist and singer, performing around the folk clubs and pubs in the west of Scotland. When Lynne and I married in 1983, we danced all day to the strains of a traditional folk, faux-mediaeval band from Dumfriesshire. I got to know traditional singers like Heather Heywood and worked with them, but more importantly, I listened carefully to them sing and became aware of the deep reservoir of songs that they had on tap, and of their performance techniques. I also listened attentively especially to the pipers and fiddlers I worked with. I believe that these were the central experiences which shaped the mood and emotion of the outer sections in the *Confession*.

Another piece from that time, a piano concerto *The Berserking*, written for Peter Donohue and the RSNO in 1989, attempted to grapple with various aspects of the Scottish character, and even of local political tendencies, through the prism of the style of Scottish football. A heady time indeed! A lot was going on in my head, and it was being channelled into my music. I felt fecund. As was Lynne, literally, being pregnant with our first child, Catherine – who developed the nickname 'The Berserker' as she kicked and punched energetically inside her mother during pregnancy. When *The Confession of Isobel Gowdie* was premiered in the Albert Hall in August 1990, just a month before the birth, she again went berserk in the womb, responding to the aural and visceral convulsions on the stage a few metres away. Catherine was born on 22 September, the very day *The Berserking* premiered at the Music Nova festival in Glasgow.

Tryst, The Confession of Isobel Gowdie and *The*

Berserking, all composed in the late 1980s, were instrumental and secular works. But something else was stirring too in my mind at this time – there was an itch about music and the sacred, a hunch that religious music could indeed still be composed in the late twentieth century, albeit from a different mindset and in a variety of new ways. The world had changed, but some things remain, eternally.

Chapter 4

The Search for the Sacred

One of the big surprises in my creative life has been the wider recognition that the spiritual inspirations behind the great composers, past and present, springing from Judeo-Christian civilisation, should be seriously reassessed. By this, I don't mean in some reductive, anthropological detachment from the sources, which amounts to a de facto denial of the theological and cultural claims of that tradition, or an implied, haughty downgrading of its authenticity. Rather, the reassessment is a recognition of the potency of a culture with Christ very much at its origin and centre, and a joyous sense of wonder at everything that has flowed from it in centuries of music-making. What brings this recognition and reassessment some urgency is the wider, sometimes reluctant concession that religion has played a huge part in musical modernity from Wagner to the present day. Some of the world's most important composers were profoundly religious people. Not all were necessarily conventional believers, and many were not Christian, but the search for the sacred has been constant and widespread in musical modernity.

When I speak about this phenomenon, some are surprised that Wagner figures so centrally at the beginning of the process. His religious faith was shaky at best, sometimes all over the place between Lutheranism and a late discovery of Buddhism (with a strange Eucharistic detour in *Parsifal*), and he was sometimes decidedly anti-clerical. But Wagner was deeply significant in the twentieth century's search for the sacred in its art music, as Roger Scruton argues in his controversial and provocative book *Death-devoted Heart – Sex and the Sacred in Tristan and Isolde*. 'Even if Wagner the man made no place for religion, however,

Wagner the artist was entirely given over to it,' he writes. 'What we see on the stage and hear in the music are human beings steeped in a religious form of life, surrounded by supernatural powers, and living, as it were, on the threshold of the transcendental.' And Michael Tanner, in his 1996 book on the composer, describes *Tristan and Isolde* – and not *Parsifal*, with its big Holy Communion scenes – as one of 'the two greatest religious works of art of our culture' (the other being Bach's *St Matthew Passion*). It turns out there is a 'eucharistic' scene in Act One of *Tristan and Isolde* too, when, through drinking potion from a chalice, the two protagonists are lost to love; they fall in love with each other, but, more importantly, also allow themselves to be given over to the power of an all-consuming numinous force. The love is erotic and pagan in its original storytelling, but the wider implications in Wagner's music drama are hugely cosmic. The original mythology is channelled through Schopenhauer and Freud, and the Christian essence is shrouded and seemingly out of sight. But for Scruton the implications and symbolism are massive. Pessimism, fate and the search for the existential oblivion of the self into the eternal embrace of divine love – all imply contradictions of Judeo-Christianity as well as metaphors and signals towards it too. This is what fascinates Scruton, whose simultaneous search for sex and the sacred in this masterwork is so compelling and disturbing to believer and sceptic alike. For Wagner, it is all about the primacy of myth, which, for him, is not merely fables and fairy stories, and certainly not religious doctrine, but rather a vehicle of human knowledge. As Scruton writes, 'Myths do not speak of what was but of what is eternally. They are magical-realist summaries of the actual world, in which the moral possibilities are personified and made flesh.'

Wagner's impact on modern literature, art and music was huge. His ritualistic, quasi-liturgical symbolism impacted on Strauss and Schoenberg as well as writers such as Thomas Mann, James Joyce and T.S. Eliot. Even Wagner's detractors and avoiders, observes Scruton, came under the spell in their reaction to his work. Bartók, Stravinsky, Debussy, Pound, Cocteau, Matisse, Rodin and Picasso, argues Scruton '[all] reveal a renewed interest in the sacred as a dominant human fact'. Wagner's colossal presence is still central, and the search for the sacred is clearly very much a current concern in contemporary composition. It never went away, and probably never will.

Major modernist composers of the last hundred years were, in different ways, profoundly religious men and women. Igor Stravinsky was as conservative in his religion as he was revolutionary in his musical imagination, with a deep love of his Orthodox roots as well as the Catholicism he encountered in the West. He set the psalms, he set the Mass; he was a man of faith. Schoenberg, that other great polar figure of early twentieth-century modernism, was a mystic who reconverted to Judaism after he left Germany in the 1930s. His later work is infused with Jewish culture and theology, and he pondered deeply on the spiritual connections between music and silence. It is no surprise that John Cage chose to study with him. Cage found his own route to the sacred through the ideas, and indeed the religions, of the Far East. It is intriguing that his famous, or indeed notorious *4'33"* (that is, four minutes and thirty-three seconds of silence), a profound provocation to our listening culture and sensibilities or lack of them, was originally entitled *Silent Prayer*.

There are, in my view, two composers in history who may be described as theologians: one is J.S. Bach and the other is the great French innovator and individualist Olivier Messiaen. Messiaen, who wrote one opera – *Saint François d'Assise* – was famously Catholic, and every note of his unique contribution to music was shaped by a deep religious conviction and liturgical practice. Messiaen was a powerful influence on major postwar avant-garde composers such as Boulez and Stockhausen and therefore can be counted as one of the most impactful composers of modern times. His Catholicism, far from being an impediment, was the major – indeed, singular – factor behind his genius, his modernism and his individuality.

But arguably the most important French Catholic opera of the twentieth century, and indeed probably the most successful modern opera of the last sixty years, was written by Francis Poulenc. His *Dialogue des Carmélites* premiered in 1957. As the American Jesuit Mark Bosco comments, 'No other opera combines 20th-century musical sensibilities with such profound theological themes on Catholic mysticism, martyrdom, and redemption.' There is no comfortable, airy-fairy, pick 'n' mix spirituality here. Based on a true story from the beginnings of modern revolutionary violence – that of sixteen Carmelite nuns guillotined in the terror of the French Revolution – the opera was an act of defiance on the part of the composer against the secular terror of that time and the secular orthodoxies of the modern world. For a culture that was meant to have put these old things behind it, *Dialogue des Carmélites* is a bold rebuttal of secular arrogances and certainties, and a beautiful proclamation of Catholic truths. Here, as Bosco highlights, 'traditional Catholicism becomes intellectually compatible with all that was modern and progressive in French culture in the early part of the twentieth century'. Poulenc's opera is 'at once a Catholic story of heroism and faith and yet speaks to the modern world, an opera for the postwar period of Europe in the 1950s and one resonant with our contemporary struggle with Christian faith and martyrdom'.

The list of composers in recent times radiating a high degree of religious resonance is substantial, covering a whole generation of post-Shosta-kovich modernists from behind the old Iron Curtain including Henryk Górecki from Poland; Arvo Pärt from Estonia; Giya Kancheli from Georgia; Valentyn Sylvestrov from Ukraine; Alfred Schnittke, Sofia Gubaidulina and Galina Ustvol-skaya, all from Russia – again, courageous figures who stood out and against the prevailing dead-hand orthodoxy of the day, state atheism. And, in the United Kingdom, after Benjamin Britten have come Jonathan Harvey, John Tavener and many others. Far from being a spent force, religion has proved to be a vibrant, animating principle in modern music and continues to promise much for the future. It could even be said that any discussion of modernity's mainstream in music would be incomplete without a serious reflection on the spir-itual values, belief and practice at work in com-posers' minds.

This artistic context and reading of cultural history has given me much sustenance and encouragement, and I have had the confidence and inspiration to compose a series of works, choral and instrumental, which have sprung out of theological and liturgical reflections. Among the most significant of these for me was *Seven Last Words from the Cross*, which I composed in 1993. It was one of my earliest pieces to engage with the Passion and death of Christ, which is a theme I have revisited in various very different ways in the years since. I have been circling these few violent days in human history again and again, and music seems to flow out of this experience. After *Seven Last Words* (which is for choir and string orchestra) came 'abstract' instrumental works such as *Fourteen Little Pictures* (for piano trio) and a triptych of orchestral works entitled *Triduum*, based on the three days before the Resurrection.

In June 1993, just before I wrote *Seven Last Words*, my twins, Aidan and Clare, arrived in this life. Lynne and I now had three kids all under the age of three. We gave up sleeping for a few years. It made the experience of composing feel rather fevered for some time, and I actually wrote more music, not less. I remember writing *Seven Last Words*, *Epiclesis* (a huge trumpet concerto) and

67

Here In Hiding (for the Hilliard Ensemble) with one or other of the twins strapped to my front as Lynne dealt with the other one.

In 1994, in the middle of all this exhausting but joyful chaos I headed to the Kennedy Center in Washington, D.C. to hear the US premiere of my percussion concerto played by Evelyn Glennie with the American National Symphony Orchestra and conducted by Mstislav 'Slava' Rostropovich, the great Russian cellist. This was to be a significant encounter. Slava seemed to take us to his heart, and he invited Evelyn and me to his Washington apartment one night for a scrumptious dinner prepared by his wife, the famous soprano Galina Vishnevskaya. His table chat – life stories of the people he had met and worked with – was one moment hilarious, the next astonishing. As well as working with great composers such as Shosta-kovich, Prokofiev and Britten, he had first-hand experience of Stalin, Brezhnev, Sakharov, Solzhen-itsyn and the Kennedys, although his favourite American president was Reagan. The next morning, he told us, he was going to Dulles Airport to pick up his old friend Eduard Shevardnadze, who had been Gorbachev's foreign minister and was then the president of Georgia.

Slava had fled the USSR in 1974, given an impromptu performance at the fall of the Berlin Wall in 1989 and returned home a few years later to show support for democracy when the communists attempted their post-Glasnost coup in Moscow in 1991. He showed us a photograph of himself under siege in the Moscow White House, holding the Kalashnikov of a young soldier sleeping against his shoulder. Evelyn and I were open-mouthed at all this.

In the midst of the dinner, he invited me to write him a cello concerto and my first symphony. These two works became parts two and three of the aforementioned *Triduum*, commissioned by the London Symphony Orchestra in the late 1990s. Slava gave the premiere of the concerto (which is the Good Friday piece of the triptych) with the LSO, conducted by Sir Colin Davis, in 1996, and then conducted the symphony *Vigil* (the Holy Saturday piece) a few years later with the same orchestra. Our daughter Catherine, then aged eight, attended this premiere with us, and we have a treasured photograph of her embraced in Slava's arms after the concert.

At the premiere of the cello concerto in 1996, I detected some tension between soloist and conductor. Slava and Colin Davis seemed to be from different musical universes, and as characters they were poles apart. But I liked them both, and Colin became one of my champions in his last years. After the cello concerto, he conducted quite a few of my works with the LSO, including the *Confession of Isobel Gowdie* at the BBC Proms in the Royal Albert Hall and in a commercial recording as well as *The World's Ransoming*, a concertante work for cor anglais and orchestra, and part one of *Triduum* (the Maundy Thursday piece). A few years later, he would ask me to write my St John Passion for him, which I dedicated to him as an eightieth birthday present. He also encouraged me in my conducting and always advised that it was an important and necessary counterpart to my work as a composer. I had never had a conducting lesson in my life up until then and nervously asked Sir Colin if he could give me one. He agreed, and I arrived one day at his London home with a pile of scores I was working on. He was quite reticent and didn't say much at all – apart from the odd remark here and there, but he was full of quixotic and mysterious asides that made me ponder for ages. He was more interested in getting my insights (and even conducting strategies) on my own *Confession of Isobel Gowdie*, which he was preparing for performance at the time. It was odd – it felt as if it was me who was giving him a lesson! Still, I will remember it as one of the most vital few hours in my musical education. It was never my intention as a young man to be on the podium so much, but conducting has now become a major part of my life.

I learned a lot from these wonderful musicians – Glennie, Rostropovich, Davis – and I've been blessed with the opportunities to write for them, and in some cases to work alongside them on stage. Countless other musicians since have made me grow professionally as we have shared in the life-transforming, all-encompassing joys of music-making. Further enrichment and fulfilment have come from non-musical collaborators too, such as choreographer Christopher Wheeldon, who used my orchestral piece *Tryst* for a one-act show with

the Royal Ballet, and then commissioned my
second piano concerto for New York City Ballet,
and theatre director Katie Mitchell who worked
with me and poet Michael Symmons Roberts on
our operas *The Sacrifice* for Welsh National Opera
and *Clemency* for the Royal Opera and Scottish
Opera.

Michael Symmons Roberts has been my main
and constant collaborator since the mid 1990s,
providing me with libretti, poetry to set, and inspiration in conversation and friendship. In the early
1990s, both Michael and I had both become fathers
– an overwhelming and transformative experience.
We realised that there wasn't a lot in our culture
marking parenthood, or more specifically father-
hood. We also wanted to extend the idea of sexual-
ity celebrated in popular culture and develop it in
a different context. Together we wrote *Quickening*,
which we created for the BBC Proms in the Royal
Albert Hall in 1999. It was a huge thing – for
chorus, large orchestra, children's choir and the
four voices of the Hilliard Ensemble. (I've just made
a new version of it for the six voices of the King's
Singers which will be performed at the Edinburgh

International Festival in August 2019.) The title of the piece refers explicitly to the instant of conception – 'the quickening of seed that will become ripe grain' – as well as to the moment that a woman first feels her baby kick. Exploring themes of birth, new life and new impulses, the work's three-fold vocal layers attempt to juxtapose mysticism and hyperrealism. Michael and I wanted to paint a canvas which could at one turn be intimate and private and at the next epic and celebratory. We were certainly celebrating an epic decade for us – not just the years when, with wives Ruth and Lynne, we had made our two families, but also when we had matured as poet and composer and made important discoveries about our work as religious artists in the modern age.

It was Michael who drew my attention to the etymology of the Latin word *religio* – that it implies a kind of binding. He cites the Welsh poet David Jones's essay 'Art and Sacrament':

> The same root is in 'ligament', a binding which supports an organ and assures that organ its freedom of use as part of a body.

And it is in this sense that I here use the word 'religious'. It refers to a binding, a securing. Like the ligament, it secures a freedom to function. The binding makes possible the freedom. Cut the ligament and there is atrophy – corpse rather than corpus. If this is true, then the word religion makes no sense unless we presuppose a freedom of some sort.

Relating this concept to art, Michael suggested that 'perhaps to "free the waters" and help slake the thirst of a parched culture, poets and other artists need religion, need a theology. Now there's an unfashionable idea.' Unfashionable but paradoxically liberating for both of us, both in our work together and in our separate ways. Encountering his suggestion that supreme artistic vision requires religion and theology was a lightbulb moment of discovery and clarity for me. 'If David Jones is right,' Michael writes, 'then that image of the free-spirited artist is, and always has been, an illusion. Freedom is not absence. The binding makes possible the freedom.'

The Search for the Sacred

Far from feeling isolated, restricted or peripheralised in the world of music because of religion, I have felt central in it and dynamically engaged, as a believer, with the swirl of ideas that surrounds us. The search for the sacred seems as strong now in music as it ever was. And perhaps that search – as it was with the theological rootedness of Messiaen's masterworks, as it was in Poulenc's glorious celebration of the mercy, sacrifice and redemption at the heart of Catholic teaching, as it is for any artist who stands out and against the transient fashions and banalities of the cultural mainstream – could be regarded as one of the bravest (or most foolhardy), most radical and counter-cultural searches a creative person can have today: a search for how the world around us might be re-sacralised.

Chapter 5

The Accompaniment of Silence

Silence is a composer's lot. We spend a lot of time in silence, probing what is there, in the undergrowth of our thoughts. Silence listening to silence. Music grows out of the silence of our own minds, gestates there, and comes forth.

This silent place is not necessarily a happy or contented place. Sometimes the silence is dreadful and frightening. No wonder Beethoven raged against deafness, that dying of sound. What a frightening place to travel into, for anyone who has ever heard. And what an especially vile place for a musician and composer to go to and never return from. But go he did. And in that soundless, airless vacuum of nothing, what did the composer meet? We will never know, of course, but we have messages from that deep impact, air from this harrowed, empty place that now fill our planet with sound. What became present in that ghastly absence of sound were some the greatest master-pieces a human being has ever composed.

*   *   *

When I was working on the production of my second opera *The Sacrifice* in Cardiff in 2007 with Welsh National Opera, I would rise early in the morning to compose before heading to the Wales Millennium Centre for rehearsals. I was writing my St John Passion in those early, silent sessions, and it was terrifying, mainly because of J.S. Bach, who haunts those of us foolhardy enough to consider walking in his footsteps.

Why do the Bach Passions still speak to us today? And why was the death of Jesus – rather than His joyous resurrection – the prime motiva-tion for these masterpieces? In his book *Bach's Dialogue with Modernity*, John Butt examines the

Bach Passions in the context of our contemporary fascination with glories past. Such masterpieces, he argues, provide a firm challenge to the notion that the modern world is always improving. I find the growing popularity of hearing the Bach Passions in the lead-up to the Easter season in our 'post-religious' culture intriguing and exciting.

The ritualistic recitation of Christ's crucifixion probably began in the fourth century, and the singing of the Passion narrative has been going on since the eighth century. Singing has always been central to the Church. St Augustine said that those who sing pray twice. The 'song' of the Church, Gregorian chant, can be traced back to the songs of the Temple and synagogue. It is an amazing feeling, knowing that people have been singing the Passion for at least twelve hundred years. It wasn't until the fifteenth century that more complex versions of a sung Passion began to emerge, the earliest example of a so-called motet Passion being attributed to Jacob Obrecht. Later there were famous examples by William Byrd, Orlande de Lassus and Tómas Luis de Victoria. After the Reformation, Luther's friend and collaborator Johann

Walther wrote responsorial Passions which became models for the Lutheran church. Within this environment the development of the 'oratorio' Passions of the sixteenth and seventeenth centuries paved the way for Bach.

Before I encountered any of the great Bach Passions, I was aware of the crucifixion narratives, even as a child. I'd heard them recited every year as part of the Church's liturgy. On Good Friday we would hear St John's account. Sometimes there would be a participatory aspect to the recitation, with the words of Christ being delivered by the priest and those of other characters read by deacons or lay readers.

I have taken part in chanted Passions since my undergraduate days. For years I would sing the narrator's part in an English plainsong setting of the St John Passion with a couple of Dominican friars in Glasgow; my little choir of volunteers would interject with the angry responses of the chorus. I am always awestruck at the stark, relentless nature of this way of doing it, and at the dramatic impact it has on the assembly as they relive the last hours of Christ's mortal life.

It is not just the Bach Passions that are in ongoing dialogue with modernity. The figure of Christ himself, in his death and resurrection, is in constant, uncontrollable interplay with the mind of modern humans, who, now more detached from liturgical obligations than ever before, may be able, paradoxically, to see the crucifixion in wider contexts. The 'greatest story ever told' began with a terrified Jewish girl saying yes to a heavenly manifestation which brought news of her pregnancy. Bach's music proves that the Passion of Christ has deep beginnings and profound resonance, even for modern man: he opened up a window on the divine love affair with humanity. The greatest calling for an artist, in any age, is to do the same.

A few years later I wrote a St Luke Passion, and I have an idea that I would like to set the Mark and Matthew eventually too, before I die. But there are other ways of telling this story. I seem to have grown up with the *Stabat Mater*. I sang a hymn version of it as a boy, and my perception of the crucifixion was coloured by its beauty and sadness. I eventually set it myself in 2015. The text is a thirteenth-century hymn meditating on the suffering of Mary, the mother of God, as she stands at the foot of the cross. '*Stabat Mater dolorosa/ juxta Crucem lacrimosa,/dum pendebat Filius*' ('The grieving Mother stood weeping beside the Cross where her Son was hanging') – these are the first words of a long poem, twenty stanzas in total about Mary as she beholds her dying son. For devout Catholics – and the many composers who set these words – this is a kind of ultimate, spiritual *Kindertotenlied* (a song on the death of a child). The poem goes beyond mere description. It invites the reader and the listener to partake in the mother's grief as a path to grace, and as part of a believer's spiritual journey. The suffering, broken heart of Mary is recapitulated in the lives of many, and artists with an empathy for our shared human-ity will always return to embrace it.

I first met John Studzinski, founder of the Genesis Foundation, in 2008. It was he (and Harry Christophers, founder and conductor of The Six-teen), who suggested the *Stabat Mater* for a large-scale work, prompted by his belief that Mary's grief at the foot of the cross is recognisable to hun-dreds of thousands of parents around the world, especially today, in a time of war and migrant crisis.

Engaging with this degree of tragedy, every day, in the silences of a composer's daily thoughts and work, has a huge effect on one's feelings. The heart-break clings to you. The events around my writing of the *Stabat Mater* went back to the death of my mother in 2008. She died on 27 December, the Feast of St John the Evangelist, and her Requiem Mass took place in the church of the same name in Cumnock in early January. My two daughters, Catherine and Clare, sang a Responsorial Psalm I had composed for it specially. That afternoon, Catherine, my eldest, headed off to Tanzania to work as a volunteer for a Jesuit charity in Dar es Salaam and Dodoma. She was initially teaching and then latterly caring for severely disabled children. In retrospect, it was as if she was being prepared.

She met someone there with whom she thought she would return to Scotland and marry. That didn't happen. But she did return with a little girl in her belly.

When the time came for Catherine to give birth in 2010 she was rushed to hospital, and the onset of labour was very quick. So quick that she was not able to get the usual pain-controlling support. Labour was difficult and painful. You may know that nowadays mothers are able to take their favourite music in with them to the labour suite. Catherine didn't have time to get her CDs organised but took along a portable radio. As her baby entered the world, music filled the room. BBC Radio 3 was playing my setting of 'O bone Jesu' that I had written for The Sixteen. When joy, the fear of loss, the fragility of life and inextinguishable hope were all in alignment, Catherine and her and new baby heard words which spoke of the infinite mercy of God, set to music that was not too far from home.

Catherine's baby, Sara Maria, was severely disabled and had many, many problems. Sara's condition is called Dandy-Walker Syndrome, which means that three parts of her brain did not form correctly in the womb. Her other conditions included epilepsy, cortical vision impairment, scoliosis and hip problems, and she was fed entirely through the gastrostomy tube in her stomach. She was non-verbal and immobile. She also wore hearing aids for a long time. Her first few years involved numerous emergency dashes to the hospital. Lynne and I became assistant parents to help Catherine.

Sara depended on us for everything. But what she gave back was extraordinary. She was patient and happy, coping with illness, seizures and constant setbacks with smiles and humour. She took delight in us, and in turn we delighted in her. I was overjoyed that she loved music, whether it was her mum singing to her, or the work of music therapists in her school, or just sitting on my knee at the piano as we both pounded and stroked away at the keys. She seemed to know that she was funny, and that she made us laugh.

But sadly, her life was to be brief; without warning, she passed away peacefully in her sleep, a few months before her sixth birthday.

At her Requiem Mass at St Columba's Church in Maryhill, members of Cappella Nova sang the motet I had composed for her baptism just a few years before, to this text from John's Gospel:

Think of how God loves you.

He calls you His own children,
And that is what you are.

I wrote my *Stabat Mater* in the few months approaching her death. Perhaps it was my way of preparing myself, subconsciously, for what was about to happen – I could feel something coming. Although my daughter doesn't now remember this, I recall a doctor hinting to us in the early days that Sara would not have a long life. The work was not written as a personal or family statement, though. What was more in my mind during its composition was something that John Studzinski had said to me about the poem's reach into modernity, into the lives of people now, especially of those mothers losing their children in the wars in Iraq and Afghanistan or in the upheavals of enforced flight from danger. The media images of Alan Kurdi, the three-year-old Syrian refugee boy who drowned in 2015 in the Mediterranean Sea, haunted my mind at this time.

There is so much in the crucifixion narrative that can be recapitulated in the lives of ordinary people, throughout history. It seems to be at the core of our lives, making Jesus that single figure from history that draws all human life, and death, towards him. The vision of Mary at the foot of His cross resonated in our family too.

Catherine was broken by the death of her daughter and returned to live with us in the countryside. We hunkered down and tried to help her through the fiercest grief of those early days and on into the recovery that only time can bring.

We will never get over the loss of little Sara. She changed us, and made us realise what was important in life. She taught us the true nature of love, what sanctity of life means, and very possibly what the presence of God is. She fills all our silences – with memories of smiles and delight, love and commitment, loss and pain. I'm sure it has been she, sometimes, who has infused the sounds that well up in my mind and lead to the music I've written since. In the silence, I hear her.

*   *   *

Subtitled 'Silence', my third symphony drew inspiration from the novel of the same name by one of

The Accompaniment of Silence

Japan's greatest twentieth-century writers, Shūsaku Endō, who died in 1996. His book tackles profound philosophical issues and resonates with one of the most anguished questions asked two thousand years ago: 'My God, my God, why have you abandoned me?' It is a question that has been asked continuously since, right through Auschwitz and into our own time. The silence Endō explores is the silence of God in the face of terrible events – torture, genocide, Holocaust – springing from the merciless nature of humans. One of Endō's characters writes: 'I cannot bear the monotonous sound of the dark sea gnawing at the shore. Behind the depressing silence of this sea, the silence of God [...] the feeling that while men raise their voices in anguish, God remains with folded arms, silent.'

Endō was a convert to Catholicism, and, for him, this silence is not absence but presence. It is the silence of accompaniment, of Christ accompanying us along our via dolorosa, suffering with us, as one of us, rather than *nihil*. And the notion of silence as presence, as mystical or metaphysical substance, is one that has many musical analogies. The emptiness and solitude of a composer's silence is nevertheless pregnant with the promise of possibility and potency. The immateriality of music points to the reality of different types of existence. Music is not a physical reality in the sense that we are, or any other thing is. You cannot see, touch or taste music, but its powerful presence always makes itself felt.

In an email to Erling Kagge, a Norwegian explorer and author of the 2017 book *Silence,* the playwright and author Jon Fosse wrote, 'Perhaps it's because silence goes together with wonder, but it also has a kind of majesty to it, yes, like an ocean, or like an endless snowy expanse. And whoever does not stand in wonder at this majesty fears it. And that is most likely why many are afraid of silence'. We fill our worlds with everything that will challenge, contradict and ultimately kill this precious silence. This disquiet at being alone, at holding our tongues, at being starved of distraction has been with us, all of us, from the beginning – it is our natural state. So we wage war on it. Silence is almost extinct. Music itself has been harnessed and co-opted as a weapon in this elemental war, transformed as it is into ubiquitous muzak. Musicians should not collude with this. The war against silence is also a war against ourselves and against our interior life, the source of our creativity. Descend into silence and you become an extension of it. Composers should feel the silence adhering to them.

Why do we resist going there? There is clearly a fear of nothingness – the abyss of non-being. That is completely natural. We avoid thinking about our own deaths, for example – the deep scandal of being irrelevant to this exciting, throbbing, living world. But what if there is something even more terrifying than nothing at the heart of this silence? What if Endō is right – that this silence is not absence but presence? When stoics, mystics, saints and composers dig deep into this silence searching for what is there, what if they meet something that is also searching for us?

I don't know if this is what John Cage had in mind when he devised his *4'33"*, a provocation to our listening sensibilities, or lack of them, a goad to make us hear music and other things better, a challenge perhaps to our culture of instant entertainment. As I stated earlier in this book, it may come as a surprise to some that his original title for this apparently jocular little slice of aesthetic naughtiness was *Silent Prayer*. I have read one claim that *4'33"* grew out of a chance encounter (what else?!) that Cage had in a New York church in 1952. In the modern western world, in the 1950s as well as today, one of the few places one encounters a sustained period of silence is during a performance of Cage's work, or during the Consecration of the Elements in a Tridentine (or Traditional Latin) Mass, when everything goes silent as the gifts of bread and wine are transubstantiated into the Body and Blood of Christ. This moment in the Tridentine Mass ('the Extraordinary Form' of the Mass, and now only rarely performed) is usually about four and a half minutes long . . .

*   *   *

Silence calls us composers from its depths, like a monstrous ocean. It is imperative that we obey its command. It's as simple as that. Because when all the lessons are over, when we've completed our last counterpoint exercise, when we've learned all we can about how to orchestrate, when we've studied modernism, postmodernism, minimalism, neo-complexity and 'musica negativa' until we can't think straight, there is only one other place to go. How should we travel there?

Have you ever gazed into the eyes of another person for a long time? Lovers and spouses do it. Parents and children do it. But otherwise it's weird, uncomfortable, unnatural. Twenty years ago, as Erling Kagge discusses in *Silence*, the psychologist Arthur Aron conducted an experiment. He was able to get complete strangers to fall in love in his laboratory. After answering some increasingly personal questions, the participants had to sit and look into each other's eyes for four minutes (or maybe four minutes thirty-three seconds!) without saying a word. Two of the subjects were married six months later.

In 2015 the *New York Times* journalist Mandy Len Catron described those four silent minutes of nothing – nothing but eye contact – as 'thrilling and terrifying':

> I know the eyes are the windows to the soul
> or whatever, but the real crux of the moment

was not just that I was really seeing someone, but that I was seeing someone really
seeing me. Once I embraced the terror of
this realisation and gave it time to subside, I
arrived somewhere unexpected.

In this scenario, four minutes becomes a very long
time – it is as though one is being pulled towards
the other. I sometimes thought about this when I
stared into the eyes of my little granddaughter
Sara. She had cortical vision impairment, but her
eyes were beautiful and didn't seem defective. She
would stare back at us with delight. Silently. One
doctor told me, 'She probably does see, but not like
we see.'

Looking at Sara, I sometimes think, was perhaps like gazing silently into the eyes of an icon.
Doing so is meant to let us see into the beauty of
the divine presence; the icon's eyes become
windows into the soul of God. And God looks back.
Some of the most powerful representations of the
nature of Heaven depict the Father staring into the
eyes of the Son, forever.

I'd give my life, health and wealth to be able to

stare back into Sara's eyes again. If not for eternity, then four minutes thirty-three seconds would do nicely, thank you. It was like rapture gazing at rapture, tenderness gazing at tenderness, devotion gazing upon devotion, worship gazing at worship, the cherisher cherishing the cherished, the enchanter enchanting the enchanted, heart lost to heart.

Silence listening to silence.

Acknowledgements

Sections of this book have previously appeared in article form in *Standpoint* magazine. Further details of works cited and quoted is as follows:

Chapter 1
p. 29. Aidan Nichols' book *The Art of God Incarnate: Theology and Image in Christian Tradition* was published by Darton, Longman and Todd, 1980.

Chapter 2
p. 35. David Goodhart's book *The Road to Somewhere: The Populist Revolt and the Future of Politics* was published by C. Hurst & Co., London, 2017.

Chapter 3
p. 45–6. Some of the discussion about Boulez first appeared in a *Guardian* article by the author (20 December 2003) about Boulez' book *Boulez on Conducting* (Faber, 2003).

Acknowledgements

p. 48. The note by Schoenberg about Charles Ives was found posthumously among his papers in 1953.

p. 51. The quotation by George Steiner is from the Preface to his book *Language and Silence: Essays 1958–1966* (Faber, 1967).

p. 51. The quotation by Theodor Adorno is from his book *Negative Dialektik*, originally published in 1966 (trans. E.B. Ashton, Routledge, 1973).

pp. 51–2. Alasdair MacIntyre's discussion of the Enlightenment can be found in his book *After Virtue* (University of Notre Dame Press, 1981).

pp. 54–5. Some of the discussion of *The Confession of Isobel Gowdie* appears in *MacMillan Studies*, ed. George Parson and Robert Scholl (Cambridge University Press, 2019).

Chapter 4
pp. 60–1. Roger Scruton's book *Death-devoted Heart – Sex and the Sacred in Tristan and Isolde* was published by Oxford University Press, 2003.

p. 61. Michael Tanner's description of *Tristan and Isolde* is taken from his book *Wagner* (Princeton University Press, 1996).

pp. 65–6. Mark Bosco's discussion of Poulenc's *Dialogue des Carmélites* can be found in 'Georges Bernanos and Francis Poulenc: Catholic Convergences in Dialogues of the Carmelites', *Logos* 12 (Spring 2009).

pp. 73–4. The quotation from David Jones's essay 'Art and Sacrament' is found in Michael Symmons Roberts, 'Poetry in a Post-Secular Age', *Poetry Review* 98 (2008).

Chapter 5
pp. 77–8. John Butt's book *Bach's Dialogue with Modernity* was published by Cambridge University Press, 2010.

p. 87. Shūsaku Endō's novel *Silence* was originally published in 1966 (trans. William Johnston, Taplinger Pub. Co., 1980)

p. 88. Jon Fosse is quoted in Erling Kagge's book *Silence* (trans. Becky L. Crook, Penguin, 2017).

pp. 91–2. The quotation by Mandy Len Catron is taken from her article 'To Fall in Love with Anyone, Do This', *The New York Times*, 9 January 2015.